The Tomb of King Tutankhamen

UNEARTHING ANCIENT WORLDS

Michael Woods
and Mary B. Woods

Twenty-First Century Books · Minneapolis

For Marvin Coyner

Twenty-First Century Books
A division of Lerner Publishing Group, Inc.
241 First Avenue North
Minneapolis, MN 55401 U.S.A.

Website address: www.lernerbooks.com

Library of Congress Cataloging-in-Publication Data

Woods, Michael, 1946–
    The tomb of King Tutankhamen / by Michael Woods and Mary B. Woods.
        p.   cm. — (Unearthing ancient worlds)
    Includes bibliographical references and index.
    ISBN 978-0-8225-7506-1 (lib. bdg. : alk. paper)
    1. Tutankhamen, King of Egypt—Tomb—Juvenile literature. 2. Excavations (Archaeology) —
Egypt—Juvenile literature. 3. Carter, Howard, 1874–1939—Juvenile literature. I. Woods, Mary B.
(Mary Boyle), 1946– II. Title.
    DT87.5.W66 2008
    932'.014—dc22   2007025331

Manufactured in the United States of America
1 2 3 4 5 6 – PA – 13 12 11 10 09 08

TABLE OF CONTENTS

This ceramic art from the 1340s B.C. shows King Tutankhamen as a young boy. It is located at the Egyptian Museum in Cairo.

INTRODUCTION

For hundreds of years, ancient Egypt was ruled by kings and queens called pharaohs. Many of Egypt's pharaohs became famous in history.

King Djoser (about 2650–2575 B.C.) built the first pyramids—the enormous stone tombs that rise out of Egypt's desert sands. Queen Hatshepsut (1479–1458 B.C.) was the first woman pharaoh. She sent expeditions to other countries to open up trade routes. Ramses II (1271–1213 B.C.) was a great military general. Other pharaohs were great thinkers, builders, and warriors.

The future pharaoh Tutankhamen was born about 1343 B.C. By that time, pharaohs had ruled Egypt for more than 1,600 years. Tutankhamen was born into the eighteenth dynasty (family of rulers) of pharaohs. Egypt was a rich and powerful nation then, with influence throughout the Middle East and central Africa.

Tutankhamen became pharaoh about 1334 B.C. He was just nine years old. At that age, he

This figurine of a young Tutankhamen is a gilded wood *ushabti* from 1332–1322 B.C. Ushabtis were figurines designed to accompany the deceased in their tombs.

did not really rule Egypt. All pharaohs had advisers called viziers. Tutankhamen's vizier, Ay, made most of the decisions about how to run the country.

As Tutankhamen grew up, he probably began ruling on his own. But the "boy king" did not have much time to make a name for himself as a great leader. Tutankhamen died young in about 1325 B.C. He had ruled for less than ten years. Egyptians at the time would have been amazed to learn that Tutankhamen would someday be the world's most famous pharaoh.

KING TUT'S TOMB

After Tutankhamen died, his body was mummified. In mummification the skin, bones, and other parts of a body are preserved. Tutankhamen's mummy was then placed in a tomb in Egypt's Valley of the Kings.

This modern photo shows Egypt's Valley of the Kings.

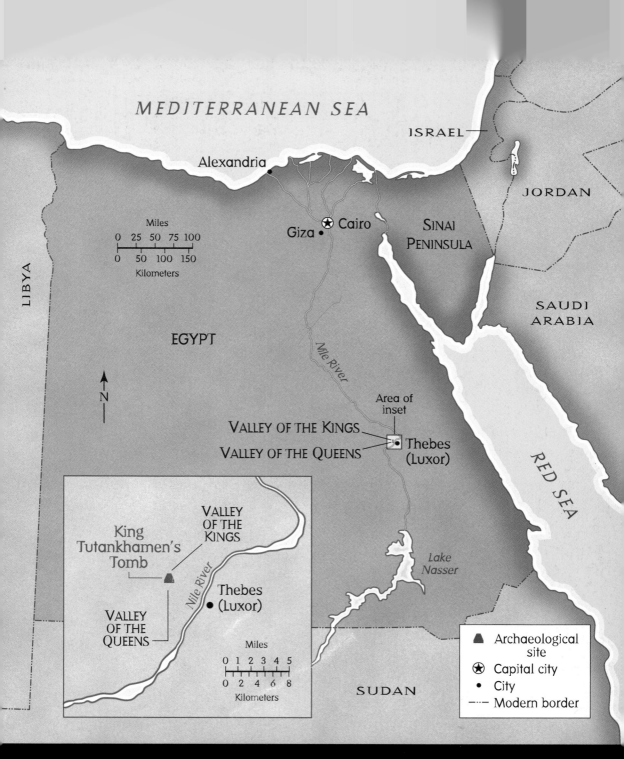

The ancient Egyptians buried their pharaohs in the Valley of the Kings. Pharaohs' wives were buried in the nearby Valley of the Queens. Archaeologists (scientists who study buildings and artifacts to help understand ancient culture) have named each tomb using

The valley is a desert area across the Nile River from the ancient Egyptian capital city of Thebes (modern-day Luxor). Eventually, people forgot all about Tutankhamen.

After more than three thousand years, however, Tutankhamen became famous. He became as much a symbol of ancient Egypt as the pyramids. In fact, he is the only pharaoh popular enough to have a nickname. People everywhere know him as King Tut. How did King Tut become the superstar of this great ancient civilization?

King Tut became famous because of his tomb. Following ancient religious traditions, Egyptian pharaohs were buried with gold, jewels, and other fantastic treasures.

In modern times, scientists called archaeologists began to study ancient Egyptian culture and history. Archaeologists study buildings and artifacts to help understand an ancient culture. Artifacts are tools, weapons, toys, and other objects left behind by a civilization. By studying those objects, archaeologists can learn about life in antiquity (ancient times).

Archaeologists hoped that some objects from the pharaohs' tombs would help them understand ancient Egyptian religion. Artwork from the tombs could reveal what the Egyptians valued and admired. Simpler artifacts such as pottery and furniture could show what everyday life in Egypt was like.

But when archaeologists opened many of the tombs, they found that much of the treasure and many artifacts were gone or damaged. Over the centuries, the treasure-filled tombs had attracted

FAST FACTS ABOUT KING TUT

- King Tut became Egypt's pharaoh about 1334 B.C., when he was nine years old.
- At the time of King Tut's rule, Egypt was a wealthy and powerful country.
- King Tut ruled for just ten years. He died about 1325 B.C. at the age of eighteen.
- After death, Egyptian pharaohs were mummified and buried in tombs with rich treasures of gold and jewels.
- King Tut's tomb was in the Valley of the Kings, a desert area in southern Egypt.
- Archaeologist Howard Carter discovered King Tut's tomb in A.D. 1922—more than 3,000 years after Tut's death.

> "We might say with truth that the one outstanding feature of [Tutankhamen's] life was that he died and was buried."
>
> —Howard Carter, the archaeologist who discovered King Tut's tomb in 1922

Howard Carter was a British archaeologist who was very interested in the history of ancient Egypt.

gangs of thieves. The thieves broke into most of the pharaohs' tombs, stealing the treasures and selling them for money.

King Tut's tomb was different, however. In A.D. 1922, the British archaeologist Howard Carter discovered the tomb. As he explored inside, he saw that thieves had barely touched it. It was the first undisturbed pharaoh's tomb ever found. What Carter discovered would make him—and King Tut—famous around the world.

This wall painting from a tomb in Egypt's Valley of the Kings shows an ancient Egyptian funeral procession along the Nile River.

CHAPTER one

FROM BOY TO MUMMY

Wheat ripens in the hot sun along the Nile River in 1325 B.C. Young children chase squawking chickens and play outside their mud-brick homes. Older children help their parents with the chores. It seems like just another January day in ancient Egypt.

In the distance, sunlight reflects off the royal palace. The pharaoh Tutankhamen and the royal family live there. *Pharaoh* means "great house" in the ancient Egyptian language.

The palace is huge, and the royal family lives well. All day long, oxen pull wagons along the dusty road toward the palace. Those wagons carry fat geese, the finest fruit and vegetables, and other food for the royal family.

DEATH OF A KING

Suddenly, the sound of a trumpet fills the air. The ground rumbles as horse-drawn chariots rush toward the palace. Soldiers with swords and spears line up at the palace gates. Curious people gather along the road to watch.

The trumpeting gets louder as a special chariot leaves the palace. Soldiers move aside to let it pass. Riding in the chariot is a trumpeter and an announcer. The announcer shouts a few words that explain all the activity.

"The falcon has flown up to heaven," he shouts. "The falcon has flown up to heaven. The falcon has flown up to heaven."

The air fills with the shrieks and cries of the people. To the ancient Egyptians, the falcon is the symbol of Horus, the god of the sky. They believe that the pharaoh is a living version of Horus. The announcement means that Tutankhamen is dead.

People cannot believe that the pharaoh is dead. King Tutankhamen was only eighteen years old. The people were used to seeing the king driving off in his chariot to hunt lions, leopards, and ostriches. He always looked so strong and handsome.

AFTERLIFE

The death of a pharaoh is an emergency because of what ancient Egyptians believe about death. They believe that each person has a physical part (the body) and a nonphysical part (the spirit). They believe in an afterlife—life after death. In the afterlife, people need their bodies. The body is the place where the spirit of a person lives on for eternity.

Egyptians believe very strongly that the living must help prepare the dead for the afterlife. In the case of a pharaoh, a successful journey to the afterlife is even more important. If a pharaoh's body and spirit could not live on in eternity, it could mean disaster for his kingdom.

The journey to the afterlife begins with two ideas—the *ka* and the *ba*. The *ka* is like a life force—the power that keeps each person alive. The *ba* is a person's uniqueness. It is close to the modern idea of personality.

Egyptians believe that a person's ba separates from the body at death. The ba is described as a bird with a human head. While a person's body is being mummified and prepared for the afterlife, the ka

This bronze statue of Horus, the god of the sky, is from Egypt ca. 800 B.C.

This painting from a wooden chest in Tutankhamen's tomb shows him wearing a crown and riding in a chariot.

rests. But the ba flies to another world each day. Each night the ba flies back to the dead body. When the mummified body is ready, the ka and the ba reunite.

When the ba, the ka, and the mummified body reach the afterlife, the dead person can enjoy the afterlife. This person, born again into the afterlife, is called the *akh*.

A TOMB FOR KING TUT

King Tut's priests rush to mummify his body. Animals and plants quickly decay when they die. Bacteria (germs) use dead bodies as food. Within a few days, a body looks very different than it did during life. Eventually, a dead body looks like a skeleton with only the bones remaining. The hot weather in Egypt makes things decay rapidly, so the priests must work fast. But mummification still takes seventy days.

That gives workers some time to find a tomb. Workers start building a pharaoh's tomb as soon as he becomes king. The tombs are usually very large, with several chambers (rooms). They take years to build. But King Tut dies so young that his tomb is not ready. His followers may have to put King Tut into a smaller tomb already built for another person.

Making a Mummy

Ancient Egyptian mummy makers started by cutting into the side of King Tut's body. They scooped out King Tut's lungs, stomach, liver, intestines, and other organs. If left inside, these organs would have decayed. The decay would have destroyed the entire body. The mummy makers did not remove the heart. Ancient Egyptians believed the heart was the most important organ and had to be left in place.

King Tut's brain was also removed. The mummy makers had a special way to remove brains. They poked a hooklike tool up King Tut's nose. The hook grabbed the brain. The mummy makers swished the tool around. It mashed King Tut's brain into mush, which they then pulled out through King Tut's nose.

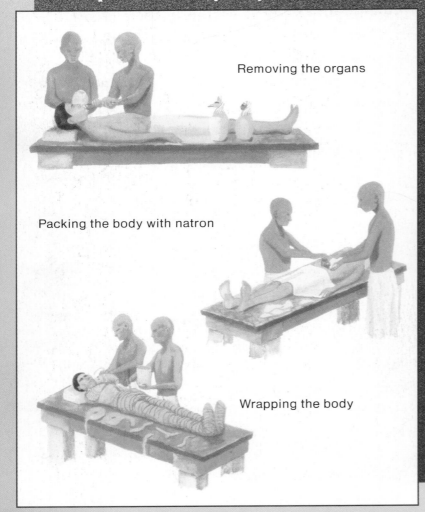

Removing the organs

Packing the body with natron

Wrapping the body

These illustrations show ancient Egyptian priests preparing a body for mummification.

Mummy makers kept King Tut's stomach, lungs, and other organs. They believed a person would need those organs to live after death. But they destroyed the brain. They did not believe it was an important organ. In ancient times, people did not understand that the brain controls physical and mental activity.

A Dash of Salt

Next, the mummy makers packed a special salt called natron around King Tut's body. Natron dried and preserved the body by drawing out liquid. Nothing was thrown away—not even the yucky liquid.

Workers also preserved the organs with salt. Then they put the organs into special covered vessels called canopic jars. The canopic jars and jars with the liquid went into King Tut's tomb.

After forty days in the salt, King Tut's body was as dry and shrunken as a prune. Workers wanted to give the mummy a more lifelike shape. So they stuffed the insides with cloth soaked in oils and spices.

Wrapping the Mummy

Priests wrapped long strips of cloth around the outside of the mummy. Layer after layer of those strips returned King Tut's body to a more lifelike size. The priests placed jewels and charms between the cloth layers to scare away evil spirits.

After the mummy was all wrapped up, workers placed a golden mask over its head. The mask showed how King Tut looked when he was alive. The mask helped King Tut's ba find his body. Finally, the mummy went into a special coffin. This wooden case had the shape of a person. The first coffin went into a bigger coffin, and then both went into a still bigger coffin. All three were then placed into a large stone coffin called a sarcophagus. King Tut was ready for his tomb.

As the priests work on King Tut's mummy, hundreds of other people rush to prepare everything that the pharaoh will need in the afterlife. Pharaohs are buried with food and with almost everything else they used while alive. For King Tut, that means gold, jewels, furniture, clothing, his royal throne, chariots for hunting, games, and other objects.

TUTANKHAMEN'S WIFE

The dead pharaoh's wife, Ankhesenamen, is sad that she has lost her husband. She is also worried about what will happen next. She and Tutankhamen do not have a son or daughter who can become the new pharaoh. Ankhesenamen worries that other powerful people in the kingdom will try to take the throne.

Some people whisper that the vizier, Ay, killed King Tut in order to become king. Ankhesenamen is also afraid of Horemheb, the leader of the army. What if Horemheb uses his soldiers to take over the palace?

Ankhesenamen decides she wants to become queen and rule Egypt herself. For that, she needs a new husband who will help her keep control of the country. So Ankhesenamen writes a

This Egyptian art shows a teenaged Tutankhamen on his throne (left) with his wife, Ankhesenamen. The artwork is at the Egyptian National Museum in Cairo.

letter to Suppiluliumas, the king of the Hittites. The Hittite kingdom is large and powerful. It occupies lands spread across modern-day Turkey, Syria, and Iraq.

"They say you have many sons," Ankhesenamen writes to Suppiluliumas. "So give me one of yours! He will be my husband, and he will be king of Egypt."

Suppiluliumas agrees to send his son Zannanza to marry Ankhesenamen. But Zannanza is killed before he reaches Egypt. Rumors spread that Horemheb had Zannanza murdered.

With nowhere else to turn, Ankhesenamen marries Ay. Ay becomes the new pharaoh before King Tut is even buried in his tomb.

What Happened to Ankhesenamen?

After marrying Ay, Ankhesenamen disappeared from history. Ancient Egyptian records do not mention her again. When Ay died, Horemheb became pharaoh. He tried to destroy all traces of King Tut, Ankhesenamen, and Ay. Horemheb had Tutankhamen and Ay removed from the official list of pharaohs.

INTO THE VALLEY OF THE KINGS

When everything for the burial is ready, the funeral parade begins. The parade takes King Tut to his tomb in the Valley of the Kings. No one lives in this remote and empty area. Egyptians have been burying their pharaohs in the valley for hundreds of years. Pharaohs no longer order pyramids to be built as their tombs. The pharaohs know that the enormous pyramids made easy targets for thieves. The thieves had little respect for the sacred burial sites and would empty tombs of their treasures. Some thieves even tore apart pharaohs' mummies to steal jewels wrapped inside.

Instead, Egyptians bury their pharaohs in secret chambers dug deep into the rock below the desert. Workers hide the entrance tunnel with sand and rock. Some people say the royal family then kills the workers so they will not tell anyone the tomb's location.

But this secrecy still does not stop many of the thieves. They eventually rob the tombs of all the pharaohs in the Valley of the Kings—all, that is, except one.

In this photo from about 1900, tourists climb on two ancient colossi (huge statues) near Lake Nasser in southern Egypt. Tourism to Egypt soared in the early 1900s, as westerners learned about archaeological discoveries there.

CHAPTER two

CLUES IN THE VALLEY

Theodore Davis wipes sweat from his face. The air feels wet and heavy. He is inside a tomb carved into rock deep below the ground. A tunnel dug into the ground leads into the tomb. Davis is a famous archaeologist working in the Valley of the Kings in the early 1900s. He is digging to find the tombs of ancient Egyptian pharaohs.

TOMB WRITERS

Davis raises the lantern higher. The light flickers off the walls of the tomb. Shadows appear like ghosts as he moves. Davis shakes his head and sighs deeply. Written there on the wall in Greek and Latin is graffiti. These drawings and words that people thoughtlessly scribble on walls are hundreds of years old.

People in ancient Greece and Rome knew about the Valley of the Kings. They visited these tombs as tourists. First, grave robbers in ancient Egypt broke in and stole things. Then people from other civilizations tramped through carelessly. All did damage to the pharaohs' burial sites.

In modern times, the Egyptian government made laws to stop the damage. The laws require people to get government permission to dig in

Egyptian workers help at an archaeological excavation near Thebes (modern-day Luxor) in the late 1800s

the Valley of the Kings. Most of that digging is now done by archaeologists.

Archaeologists must dig deep, because these tombs are hidden under piles of rock and sand. Digging is slow, hard work in this desert area. Temperatures often rise above 100°F (38°C). Huge cobras (poisonous snakes) sometimes hiss and sway at the workers.

Hundreds of men and boys help Davis and other archaeologists dig. These workers shovel sand and rocks into baskets. Then they carry the baskets away to dump them.

Everyone works so fast that an excavation site looks almost like an anthill. Workers hurry to earn more money. Their pay depends on the number of baskets they carry and dump.

CLUES, CLUES, CLUES

Davis has been excavating in the Valley of the Kings since 1902. During five years of digging, he has discovered more than thirty tombs. One is the tomb of Queen Hatshepsut. Another is the tomb of the great pharaoh Thutmose IV. Unfortunately, grave robbers from ancient times had beaten Davis to each of the tombs. The tombs are empty.

In 1907 Davis and his team are digging near the tomb of Ramses VI.

"At the depth of 25 feet [7.6 meters] we found a room filled almost to the top with dried mud, showing that water had entered it," he writes in his notebook.

Digging around this room, workers find a piece of golden foil. King Tut's name is on the foil. The archaeologists also find pictures showing King Tut hunting in a chariot.

Hieroglyphs appear near the pictures. Hieroglyphics is a system of writing that uses pictures and symbols instead of letters. The hieroglyphs near King Tut's pictures read, "All protection of life is behind him, like the sun." The message shows that at the time it was written, King Tut was already dead. Nearby, workers also find jars, cups, and cloth with King Tut's name on them. Davis is sure that this is King Tut's tomb.

By 1914 Davis has tired of excavating the valley. With the discovery of what he thinks is King Tut's tomb, Davis decides that there is nothing left to find here. "The Valley of the Kings is now exhausted [has no more tombs]," says Davis. He stops working there.

This example of hieroglyphic writing is from the tomb of Seti I in the Valley of the Kings. The hieroglyphs (pictures and symbols) stand for sounds or simple ideas. Read in order, the hieroglyphs explain bigger ideas or form sentences.

A FRIEND WITH MONEY

Another archaeologist thinks Davis is wrong about the Valley of the Kings. That archaeologist is Howard Carter. Carter had started digging in Egypt in 1891 when he was only seventeen years old.

Carter keeps track of all the tombs that Davis and other archaeologists find in the Valley of the Kings. He knows that Davis's mud-filled room was not large enough to be a pharaoh's tomb. It could have been a storeroom used during the building of the tomb. The ancient Egyptians often built storage rooms near tombs. But the room isn't, Carter knows, the tomb itself.

Carter believes King Tut's tomb remains to be discovered in the valley. Carter gets permission from the Egyptian government to dig there.

Excavations cost a lot of money. Archaeologists have to buy equipment and hire workers. They have to pay for their own place to live while at the site. Carter is not a rich man. But he knows someone who is.

Lord Carnarvon is a wealthy member of the British nobility (a very high social class). Lord Carnarvon lives at Highclere Castle in Hampshire, England. He is very interested in archaeology and Egyptology (the study of ancient Egypt). Every year Lord Carnarvon travels to Egypt to escape the cold English winters. He has taken part in some archaeological digs, but he has never discovered anything of importance.

In 1917 Lord Carnarvon agrees to pay for Carter's excavations. Carter will provide the skills of an archaeologist. Lord Carnarvon will provide the money.

Lord Carnarvon is shown in a photograph from his early days of working in Egypt with Howard Carter.

GRAVE ROBBERS' CLUES

Carter knows the location of all the royal tombs ever discovered in the valley. He thinks he knows the location of the one remaining tomb. King Tut's tomb, he believes, lies near the place where Theodore Davis found the cups with King Tut's name on them.

Those cups are important clues. Carter thinks that grave robbers dropped those cups. Why didn't the robbers pick them up? Carter thinks guards caught or killed the robbers before they could steal very much. So maybe King Tut's tomb is still filled with treasures!

Early in the fall of 1917, Carter rides a donkey from his home into the Valley of the Kings. He stops near the tombs of three great pharaohs. The tombs form a triangle. The three points of the triangle are the tombs of Ramses II, Merenpath, and Ramses VI.

Somewhere within that triangle, Carter believes, is King Tut's tomb. However, the triangle covers an area almost as big as three football fields. He plans to dig down more than 10 feet (3 m) deep to search for the tomb.

Carter picks one spot to start the search. Workers lay down tracks for

Curses!

Ancient Egyptians believed in curses—statements that threaten harm or bad luck on someone. Curses written on tombs and coffins acted as warning messages. To scare away thieves, the curses promised terrible things to anyone who broke into a burial site. Those bad things included:

- "He shall die from hunger and thirst."
- "I shall seize his neck like that of a goose."
- "His years shall be diminished."
- "The priest of Hathor [an Egyptian goddess] will beat twice any of you who enter this tomb or do harm to it."
- "He shall be miserable."
- "His wife shall be taken away before his face."
- "He shall be cooked together with the condemned."

a small railroad. Then they start digging. Archaeologists in Egypt usually begin digging in autumn, when the weather is cooler. They usually stop when summer's unbearable heat arrives.

Workers carry sand and rocks to the railroad car. When it fills up, they push the car along the tracks to a distant spot. They empty the car and push it back for another load.

DIGGING UP DISAPPOINTMENT

After digging for months in 1917, Carter finds nothing. He digs for months more in 1918 and finds no trace of King Tut. He digs in 1919 and finds nothing. Carter does find some nice stone jars in 1920, but he does not find King Tut. In 1921 he again comes up empty-handed.

"We had worked for months at a stretch and had found nothing," Carter remembers. "And only an excavator [archaeologist] knows how desperately depressing that can be. We had almost made up our minds that we were beaten, and were preparing to leave the valley and try our luck elsewhere."

BAD NEWS
AT HIGHCLERE CASTLE

During the summer of 1922, Lord Carnarvon invites Carter to Highclere Castle in England. Lord Carnarvon has bad news. Enough is enough. He has

In the summer of 1922, Lord Carnarvon called Howard Carter to Highclere Castle (below) to say he would not pay for any more Egyptian excavations.

Egyptian workers search for signs of King Tut's tomb in 1922.

paid for five excavations in the Valley of the Kings. None of those excavations has turned up any valuable artifacts. Lord Carnarvon will not pay for any more work.

Carter tells Lord Carnarvon that he will continue working in the Valley of the Kings. He will pay all his expenses himself. That embarrasses Lord Carnarvon, who has so much more money than Carter. Lord Carnarvon agrees to pay for one more season of excavations.

THE LUCKY BIRD

By October, Carter is back in Egypt. He does not know many people there and worries that he will be lonely. He decides to buy a pet to keep him company. In a small shop in Cairo, he buys a yellow canary in a gold-colored cage.

Workers at Carter's house are excited when they see the bird. "It's a bird of gold that will bring good luck," they say. "This year we will find . . . a tomb full of gold."

Carter plans to begin his next excavation by digging in front of the tomb of Ramses VI. That tomb was built after King Tut's. Carter thinks that maybe the rock and sand from construction of Ramses VI's tomb covered up and hid the entrance to King Tut's tomb.

SECRET STEPS

Work starts on November 1, 1922. It is still hot in Egypt at that time of year, and the workers sweat under the desert sun. A young boy named Hussein Abdou El-Rasoul is hired to carry water to the thirsty workers.

On the morning of November 4, the water boy sits down for a rest. Idly he sweeps his hand through the sand. His fingers hit something hard right beneath the surface. It is a flat, smooth piece of stone. The boy runs to tell Carter.

Workers clear away the sand. It looks like a stone step. Excited, they clear away more sand. It *is* a step. They clear away more sand. They find another step and another. The staircase has sixteen steps leading down into the ground.

"Hardly had I arrived at work the next morning than the unusual silence, due to the stoppage of the work, made me realize that something out of the ordinary had happened, and I was greeted by the announcement that a step cut in the rock had been discovered. . . . This seemed too good to be true, but a short amount of extra clearing revealed the fact that we were actually in the entrance [to a tomb]."

—Howard Carter, *The Discovery of the Tomb of Tutankhamen*, 1923

At the bottom of the steps is a door. Is it the door to a tomb? King Tut's tomb? Or does the door open to something else—perhaps a small storage room with nothing of value? This could be a storage room for Ramses VI's tomb.

Carter's heart thumps with excitement. But he cannot just break down the door. Lord Carnarvon is paying for this work. Carter wants Lord Carnarvon to be there to watch.

In this 1922 photograph, Carter (*right*) shows Lord Carnarvon (*left*) around the site where workers found a buried staircase.

Carter has his workers shovel sand and rock back over the steps. They must hide the staircase and door from thieves. Then Carter sends a message to Lord Carnarvon, who is still in England. "At last I have made wonderful discovery in Valley," the message reads. "Re-covered same for your arrival. Congratulations." Carter can hardly wait for Lord Carnarvon to arrive from England.

Bad Luck Bird?

People say that Carter got a surprise when he returned home after discovering the sixteen steps. They say that a cobra killed and ate Carter's pet canary. Cobras are symbols of the pharaoh. People whispered that King Tut sent the cobra to kill the canary. It was a warning to stay away from King Tut's tomb. Some people said that hundreds of hissing, swaying cobras would be waiting inside the tomb. Others said that King Tut would get even meaner and take revenge in other ways.

Left to right: Lord Carnarvon; his daughter, Evelyn Herbert; and Howard Carter stand at

CHAPTER three

A Name on a Door

Within weeks Lord Carnarvon arrives in the Valley of the Kings with his daughter, Lady Evelyn Herbert. She is interested in archaeology. Carter's best assistant, Arthur Callender, also is there to help.

Workers uncover the stairway again. Excitement grows when Carter sees hieroglyphics on the bottom of the door. Could it be true? Yes! The hieroglyphs spell out a name—Tutankhamen!

It is November 26, 1922. To Carter this is "the day of days, the most wonderful that I have ever lived through."

Workers carefully remove the door. Behind it is a tunnel carved through solid rock. At the end of the tunnel, 30 feet (9 m) away from the first door, they find another door. More hieroglyphs spell out "Tutankhamen."

GIVE ME A LOOK!

Carter makes a hole in the sealed door to look inside. Hot, stale air rushes out into his face. Carter makes the hole bigger and holds a lighted candle inside.

Carter is dazzled by the sights inside. He looks and looks. Lord Carnarvon cannot wait any longer. "Let me have a look!" he says.

Lord Carnarvon peers inside the hole in the door and gasps. Evelyn pulls on his arm excitedly. She wants to look inside. Then Callender gets his turn.

TORNADO IN A TOMB

The next day, Carter makes a bigger hole in the door so they can go in. Callender passes out flashlights. Everyone scrambles into the room.

The spooky scene is like walking into someone's house without knocking. The air smells of ancient perfumes and spices. On the floor is a big bouquet of dried flowers. As they lift their flashlights, they see that the room is a terrible mess. It looks like a tornado blew through, scattering things every which way.

This view of the west side of the antechamber in King Tut's tomb shows the contents of the room strewn about at the time of discovery.

Carter realizes that the mess was not created by things falling over or falling apart through the centuries. Thieves broke into the tomb, probably thousands of years ago. They made the mess while searching for gold and jewels to steal. But they must not have gotten far. Guards must have stopped them and resealed the tomb, because the room is still filled with treasures.

"Presently, as my eyes grew accustomed to the light, details of the room within emerged slowly from the mist, strange animals, statues, and gold—everywhere the glint of gold. . . .

"I was struck dumb with amazement, and when Lord Carnarvon, unable to stand the suspense any longer, inquired anxiously, 'Can you see anything?', it was all I could do to get out the words, 'Yes, wonderful things.'"

—Howard Carter, *The Discovery of the Tomb of Tutankhamen*, 1923

With hearts pounding, Lord Carnarvon, Herbert, and Callender dash from place to place. They gasp again and again. The room's treasures would fill a whole museum. An archaeologist would be happy to find just one of these objects after digging for months.

Carter spots beautifully carved wooden chairs, a king's throne inlaid with gold, and statues of strange, monstrous animals. One is part lion, part hippopotamus, and part crocodile. King Tut's chariots are here, glistening with gold. There are two life-sized statues of a king and many other treasures.

WHERE'S THE MUMMY?

After inspecting these wonders for a while, Carter gets worried. "Presently, it dawned upon our bewildered brains that in all of this medley of objects before us there was no coffin or trace of mummy," he writes in his notebook.

This ceremonial throne was one of the items found in King Tut's tomb. The throne is inlaid with ebony, ivory, gold, and semiprecious stones.

Is this really King Tut's tomb? Maybe it's only a storage room for extra things that would not fit into the tomb. Maybe the real tomb is in a different spot. They may have to start their search all over again.

Disappointment and doubt settles over everyone. But wait a minute, Carter thinks. Maybe this is only one room in the tomb. Maybe its walls have hidden doorways that lead to other rooms with even more fantastic treasures—including King Tut's mummy.

They search the walls of the room, which Carter calls the antechamber, for more doors. Several beds and other pieces of furniture line the walls. Under one bed, Carter finds a small hole in the wall.

Carter crawls under the bed and peers through the hole. Another room! Carter calls it the annex. He spots more treasures inside—things a wealthy king would need in the afterlife. The room is stacked with games, musical instruments, stools, vases, clothing, and weapons. But like the antechamber, the annex is a mess. Thieves must have searched this room too.

On another wall, Carter and the others find traces of a door. Plaster covers a spot where thieves broke a hole in the door thousands of years ago. Guards had patched the hole. Carter knows this because the guards left marks in the wet plaster telling what they did.

Grave Games

King Tut seems to have liked to play games. Buried in the tomb, for King Tut to enjoy forever, were several senet boards. Senet was a popular ancient Egyptian board game. Senet boards from about 3500 B.C. were found in the oldest tombs in Egypt.

A game of senet *(center)* can be seen among the baskets and ceramics in the annex in King Tut's tomb.

INTO KING TUT'S TOMB

Carter sees the outline of stone blocks under the dry plaster. Callender helps Carter pry a few blocks out of the doorway. Carter shines a flashlight through the hole. The light shows a short passageway.

Carter and Callender quickly remove more of the stones to enlarge the hole. Carter slips through the hole, feet first. He disappears for a few minutes. Then he yells to the others with news. He is in a room that seems to be a burial chamber. King Tut's mummy must be here!

Hearts thumping, Lord Carnarvon and Herbert wiggle through the hole. But Callender is a large man. He cannot squeeze through the hole.

Carter is afraid to make the hole bigger. When Carter got permission to dig in the Valley of the Kings, he agreed to follow rules. Carter worries about one rule in particular.

Archaeologists promise to tell the government of Egypt if they discover a tomb filled with treasures. They promise to tell *before* they enter the tomb. That allows the government to send an official to watch. If Carter enlarges the hole, the government may find out that Carter has already entered King Tut's tomb. That could get him kicked out of the Valley of the Kings.

Carter, Lord Carnarvon, and Herbert take a quick look at the burial chamber. Then they wiggle back through the hole. Carter covers the hole with the lid of a reed basket. Arthur Callender helps them hide the other holes in the antechamber.

All four people scamper back up the sixteen steps and into the hot desert. They climb onto donkeys and ride to Carter's house. From there, Carter writes to the Egyptian government, telling about the discovery.

Now it's time for dinner and bed. Everyone is so excited that they doubt they will sleep much. They know, however, that months of work lie ahead before they can go back into the burial chamber.

This lotus blossom cup is one of the objects found in King Tut's tomb. The cup is in a floral shape, and the text on the rim says: "May your ka live; may you spend millions of

CHAPTER four

FIRST THINGS FIRST

After those first peeks into the tomb, Carter knows one thing. King Tut's tomb is one of the greatest archaeology discoveries in history. Grave robbers didn't steal everything in this tomb. It is loaded with unbelievably rich treasures from ancient Egypt.

Why doesn't Carter tell the world right now? Why doesn't he go back and explore the burial chamber? Why not open King Tut's sarcophagus and look at the mummy?

Carter worries about what might happen. The Egyptian government might get angry because Carter broke the rules. But even worse, the government could order its workers to break into the burial chamber immediately.

The workers could damage objects in the antechamber and other rooms. Those objects have a story to tell about life in ancient Egypt. They are very fragile. If objects are moved, destroyed, or stolen, parts of that story could be lost.

A MYSTERIOUS AIRPLANE

Carter and Lord Carnarvon make a plan to trick the government. They will keep their peeks into the tomb a secret. When the government workers arrive to watch, Carter and Lord Carnarvon will pretend they have not looked into the tomb. They will pretend to "discover" each room in the tomb again. By doing so, they will have time to study the objects in each room.

"The news of the discovery had spread like wildfire," Carter recalled later, "and all sorts of fanciful reports were going abroad concerning it." One rumor is that a mysterious airplane landed in the desert one night. Then it took off—loaded with treasures from King Tut's tomb.

People in Egypt start whispering about Carter. They say that Carter emptied the tomb and sent everything to England on the airplane. Carter must stop those rumors—fast.

EGYPTOMANIA

To stop the rumors, Carter and Lord Carnarvon invite people to watch them open the tomb. At the ceremony, on November 29, 1922, Carter opens the door to the antechamber. He shows people that it still is filled with treasures.

Newspaper stories give the world a case of Egyptomania. Everyone seems to be talking about King Tut. Archaeologists in the United States and other countries read about the find. Some of them volunteer to help study the tomb.

Carter needs a lot of help. This is a huge archaeology discovery. So he gathers a team of experts who will work together.

For the study to begin, workers string bright electric lights inside the antechamber. Before anyone touches anything, the archaeologists

Little Girl in the Tomb

Archaeologist Herbert E. Winlock brought his daughter, Frances, into the antechamber of King Tut's tomb. Frances, ten years old, saw the hole in the wall leading into the annex. She took a flashlight and wiggled her head and arms into the hole to take a look. "Daddy!" she cried out. "Gold! Gold! Gold!" Frances was almost hypnotized by the treasures inside. She could not tear herself away, even when her father told her to come out. Finally, Winlock pulled Frances out of the hole—by her feet.

Workers remove an object from the tomb of King Tut in 1923.

must take photographs. They want a record of how everything looks.

Photographs are very important. Some of the objects are very fragile. A touch could turn them into dust. If that happens, photos will show how the objects looked.

After photographing the entire antechamber, the archaeologists give each object an ID (identification) number. Some objects need several photographs. Boxes, for instance, get a photograph of each side and of everything inside.

PRESERVING HISTORY

After objects are photographed, workers remove them from King Tut's tomb. Each object goes into an empty tomb nearby. Carter uses this tomb as an archaeology laboratory. Workers in the lab measure, weigh, and make drawings of each object.

The archaeologists must act fast to preserve some of the objects. Changes in the air may make an object crack or fall apart. Carter learns that lesson from the first object he takes from the antechamber. It is a wooden chest filled with clothing King Tut wore as a child. The chest starts to shrink in the heat. Parts of a beautiful painting on the chest's surface peel off. Carter and his workers coat the chest with wax to save the painting.

After measuring and labeling each object, Carter wraps it in heavy cloth. This padding keeps the objects from breaking during shipment.

Workers bring up treasure from King Tut's tomb while crowds watch from above in this 1923 illustration from the French publication *L'Illustration*.

Carter ships the objects to the Egyptian Museum in Cairo. Archaeologists in that museum do more work to clean, preserve, and study the objects.

Carter has a big audience at the tomb. Hundreds of curious people gather outside to see the treasures carried out. "The tomb drew like a magnet," Carter later writes. "Visitors arrived on donkeys, in sand-carts, and in two-horse cabs and proceeded to make themselves at home in the Valley for the day."

Left: Archaeologist Arthur Mace *(standing)* and Alfred Lucas, a chemist working for the Egyptian government, examine a piece of a chariot from King Tut's tomb. *Below:* Howard Carter *(left)* and Arthur Callender *(center)*, with the help of a worker, wrap the black and gold statues in front of the burial chamber door.

> "Just now we are working on a box which contains garments and shoes all covered with beadwork. The cloth is so rotten you can hardly touch it, and the beads drop off the shoes if you look at them."
>
> —Arthur Mace, *The Discovery of the Tomb of Tutankhamen*, 1923

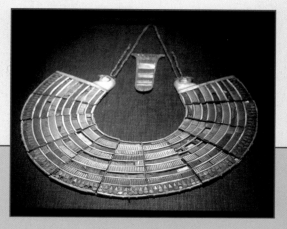

This is one of the beaded necklaces found in King Tut's tomb.

SEVEN LONG WEEKS

Clearing out the antechamber is very hard work. A single box or basket sometimes contains fifty objects. The archaeologists need a record of each and every one. Every object gets its own photographs and notes. It takes one archaeologist, Arthur Mace, almost three weeks to finish work on objects in just one wooden box.

Mace and other workers need many days to repair broken objects. Imagine necklaces of brightly colored beads strung together. The string rotted away over the years. Now nothing holds the beads together. Each bead must be restrung on the spot, so workers can follow the shape of the necklace as it lies.

Carter and his team of archaeologists work on the antechamber for seven weeks. It takes that long to clear everything out. By February everything is set for the team to enter the burial chamber.

Howard Carter *(left)* and Arthur Mace open the wall of the burial chamber in King Tut's tomb in 1922.

CHAPTER five

INTO THE BURIAL CHAMBER

The first room in King Tut's tomb looks different this day—February 17, 1923. It looks almost like a school auditorium. People in fine clothing sit in rows of chairs facing a platform built along one wall. The platform looks like a stage.

Carter and Lord Carnarvon *feel* like actors onstage. They are going to break through the wall. And behind that wall, they know, is the burial chamber that contains King Tut's mummy. Sitting in the audience are friends and other important people. When Carter and Lord Carnarvon look inside, they must act excited—as if they did not sneak into the burial chamber in November 1922.

Mervyn Herbert, Lord Carnarvon's brother, is in the audience. "The platform concealed [hid] the hole made in the wall where they had got in before," said Herbert. "[Carnarvon] poor old fellow was nervous like a naughty schoolboy fearing that [people] would discover that a hole already had been made."

AN ASTONISHING SIGHT

Lord Carnarvon makes a speech to the audience. Carter also makes a speech. Then Carter picks up a hammer and turns to the wall. "It was with a trembling hand that I struck the first blow," Carter remembers. "I chipped away the plaster and picked out the small stones which formed the uppermost layer of the filling.

"The temptation to stop and peer inside at every moment was irresistible, and when, after about ten minutes' work, I had made a hole large enough to enable me to do so I inserted an electric torch [flashlight].

"An astonishing sight its light revealed, for there, within a yard of the doorway, stretching as far as one could see and blocking the entrance to the chamber, stood what to all appearance was a solid wall of gold."

This scene showing Ankhesenamen and Tutankhamen is part of the gold shrine found inside King Tut's burial chamber.

MAGIC SYMBOLS

Callender and Mace give Carter a hand. Slowly they remove one rock after another from the wall. Sweat beads on their faces. They work slowly and carefully in the hot stone chamber. If a rock falls inward, it could damage the golden wall.

As the hole gets bigger, they see more. This is not a golden wall. It is one side of a huge wooden box covered with gold.

Carter squeezes into the burial chamber. Barely 3 feet (1 m) of space separates the chamber's stone walls and the golden box. Carter sees strange markings on the sides of the box. They are magic symbols to protect the box from thieves and evil spirits.

The box looks almost like a garden shed, with sides and a double door. Carter recognizes the box as a shrine (a holy object). This shrine must hold King Tut's mummy.

King Tut's Perfume

When archaeologists opened one beautifully made jar from King Tut's tomb, a wonderful scent escaped. The jar contained perfumed cream that was still fragrant after 3,300 years. It smelled like coconut oil.

This modern-day photograph shows one of the perfume jars found in King Tut's tomb. It is made of alabaster.

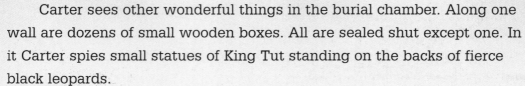

Carter sees other wonderful things in the burial chamber. Along one wall are dozens of small wooden boxes. All are sealed shut except one. In it Carter spies small statues of King Tut standing on the backs of fierce black leopards.

Suddenly, Carter remembers the audience. People are waiting in suspense in the antechamber. Carter squeezes back through the opening in the wall. He motions to the audience to take a peek. The shrine fills the burial chamber so snugly that only two people can enter at a time. Carter enjoys watching people's faces as they return to the antechamber after viewing the burial chamber. "Each had a dazed, bewildered look in his eyes," Carter remembers, "and each in turn as he came out threw up his hands before him, an unconscious gesture of [trying] to describe in words the wonders he had seen."

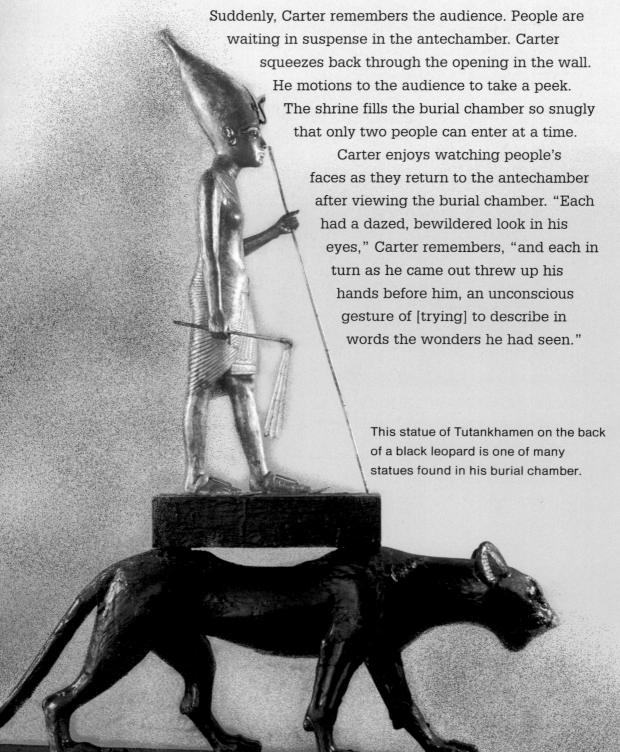

This statue of Tutankhamen on the back of a black leopard is one of many statues found in his burial chamber.

Left: The second shrine shows through the doors of the first shrine in King Tut's tomb.
Below: The second shrine doors were still locked with a clay seal when Howard Carter's team discovered them.

SHRINES NESTED INSIDE SHRINES

After the guests have viewed the burial chamber, Carter and the other archaeologists look more closely at the shrine. They discover that the seal on the shrine doors has been broken. That could mean that grave robbers got all the way into King Tut's sarcophagus. But the archaeologists are relieved when they open the doors to find another shrine inside. The doors on the second shrine have not been opened. They are still locked with an ancient clay seal.

Carter knows that the ancient Egyptians put one shrine inside another. There could be two or three more shrines nested inside. The last shrine would hold King Tut's sarcophagus. The team decides not to break the seal on the second shrine. They will wait and think about what to do next.

A statue of Anubis, the ancient Egyptian jackal god of mummification, guarded the entrance to the treasury. Behind Anubis, a golden shrine stood against the wall.

THE TREASURY

While in the burial chamber, Carter notices something else. Along the west wall is a small open doorway, low to the ground. Carter can see that this leads to another room. He squeezes down into the space and peers through the door. Just inside is a statue of Anubis, the ancient Egyptian god of mummification. Anubis took the form of a black jackal (an animal similar to a dog).

Anubis's ears are perked, and its eyes are alert as it watches the doorway. With another glance, Carter sees what Anubis is guarding. Just beyond the statue sits a golden shrine. The top of the shrine is lined with the carved heads of cobras. On each side, small statues of goddesses protect the shrine with their outstretched arms. Carter stares in amazement. He later writes that this shrine is "the most beautiful monument that I have ever seen—so lovely that it made one gasp with wonder and admiration."

The room is filled with statues meant for King Tut's protection. There are also model boats—symbols of his journey to the afterlife. Gold jewelry, pictures, and other objects are meant to make the king comfortable in the afterlife. Carter decides to call this room the treasury.

Carter and the other archaeologists want to continue their work on the burial shrines and the treasury. But they know they must wait until next autumn. Space is tight inside the burial chamber. The shrines will all have to be taken apart and their pieces removed. Otherwise, there will not be room to open the sarcophagus or explore the treasury. Removing the shrines will be heavy work, and the weather already is getting too hot. As hard as it is to wait, the team decides to leave the site until next autumn.

THE MOSQUITO THAT KILLS

The warmer weather in Egypt also brings out the mosquitoes. At the end of February, a mosquito bites Lord Carnarvon on the cheek. Lord Carnarvon swats the bug and thinks no more about it.

But when Lord Carnarvon shaves the next morning, he cuts the mosquito bite with his razor. The bite gets infected. It begins to hurt and gets red and swollen with pus. The infection spreads, and Lord Carnarvon begins running a fever. Evelyn insists he stay in bed.

After a few days, Lord Carnarvon develops pneumonia. He gets sicker and sicker. His wife, son, and personal doctor arrive from England. But they cannot help him. On April 5, 1923, Lord Carnarvon dies at the age of fifty-six. He never gets to see King Tut's mummy.

King Tut's Curse

After Lord Carnarvon died, people began to talk again about a curse on King Tut's tomb. They claimed that King Tut did not want his burial site invaded and his treasures taken away. Lord Carnarvon's death, according to this idea, was King Tut's revenge.

Newspaper stories added other odd, scary details about the curse. At the moment Lord Carnarvon died, some papers claimed, all the electric lights in Cairo went out. And back in England, Lord Carnarvon's favorite dog, Susie, howled and dropped dead. Other stories claimed that when King Tut's mummy finally was unwrapped, it had a sore on its left cheek in exactly the same place as Lord Carnarvon's mosquito bite. Newspaper stories blamed the curse for the deaths of more than thirty people.

This modern photograph shows one of the canopic jars from King Tut's tomb. The four canopic jars were used to keep King Tut's lungs, liver, stomach, and intestines. The jars were shaped like King Tut's second coffin.

CHAPTER six
KING TUT'S MUMMY

Carter returns to Egypt in the fall of 1923. He had spent the summer months back home in England. But now he is eager to begin working again on King's Tut's burial chamber. He and his team plan to clear the way so that they can remove the burial shrines. They will then be able to open King Tut's sarcophagus.

The archaeologists and workers first tear down the wall separating the antechamber and the burial chamber. They remove the boxes and other funeral objects from around the burial shrine. They are ready to begin taking the shrines apart.

PIECE BY PIECE

Carter and the other archaeologists must work slowly and carefully to take the shrines apart. No one knows how easily the pieces might break when moved. They take each shrine door off its hinges and take apart the walls.

This drawing shows workers taking apart the golden shrines around the tomb of King Tut in 1923.

This cosmetic jar from King Tut's tomb is shown here on display at the Museum of Art in Fort Lauderdale, Florida, in 2005. The jar was one of the first things Lord Carnarvon saw upon opening the burial chamber. The jar contained a mixture of plant extracts and animal fats.

The work is backbreaking. The shrines are big and heavy. The outermost shrine is almost 17 feet (5 m) long, 11 feet (3 m) wide, and 9 feet (3 m) high.

The chamber is hot and stuffy, without a breath of fresh air. Sweat soaks the archaeologists' clothing after a few minutes of work. They barely have room to move.

"We bumped our heads, nipped our fingers," Carter later remembered. "We had to squeeze in and out like weasels and work in all kinds of embarrassing positions."

As a shrine wall is removed, workers must carry it out so it does not get in the way. Each piece is awkward to handle. Workers struggle to carry the pieces up the sixteen steps and out of the tomb.

The hot, heavy work takes many weeks. But they are nearing their goal. James Henry Breasted, an archaeologist on Carter's team, remembers his first glimpse of the sarcophagus. "When Carter and I opened the doors of the third and fourth shrines and beheld the massive stone sarcophagus within, I felt for the first time the majesty of the dead pharaoh's presence."

The team takes apart the third shrine. The fourth shrine is small enough that they can lift off its roof. Inside, they see the heavy stone lid of the sarcophagus. Excitedly, they finish removing the walls to the fourth shrine.

The sarcophagus is made entirely of stone—reddish brown quartzite with a red granite lid. It is carved with strange figures and symbols. And inside lies the body of a king, unseen by anyone in more than 3,000 years.

Workers finish clearing the area around the sarcophagus by early February 1924. They begin setting up equipment to remove the heavy lid and coffin.

OPENING THE SARCOPHAGUS

On February 14, 1924, Carter walks down the sixteen steps and through the long passage into King Tut's tomb. This is a very special day. For the first time in recorded history, people will see the coffin that holds a pharaoh's body. Archaeologists will get their first glimpse of a pharaoh as he was laid to rest. Carter wishes Lord Carnarvon had lived to see this day.

Carter stands over the sarcophagus, examining its lid. The lid has a big crack in the center. Carter believes the lid probably broke during burial, as it was

Howard Carter *(kneeling at left),* Arthur Callender *(right),* and an assistant peer through the shrine doors at King Tut's sarcophagus in 1923.

being lowered over King Tut's coffins. It looks as if burial workers repaired the crack with cement. But it is still a weak spot on the heavy lid.

Carter's workers have attached ropes to the lid. They groan as they pull the ropes. The onlookers hold their breath. Will the lid break again and smash the coffin beneath?

"The sarcophagus lid trembled, began to rise," James Henry Breasted wrote later. "Slowly, and swaying uncertainly, it swung clear." With thumping hearts, everyone crowds in to see.

Carter's hands tremble as he reaches inside the sarcophagus. He moves aside two sheets of a cloth covering. The crowd gasps. Under the cloth is a magnificent wooden coffin coated in gold. The coffin is shaped like a person. Magic spells written in hieroglyphics cover the coffin's surface.

A young man's face is carved on the front. He wears the headdress of a pharaoh. Poking out from the front of the headdress are the heads of a fierce vulture and a cobra. These are symbols of the king of Upper and Lower

This drawing from 1926 shows the multiple layers of King Tut's sarcophagus.

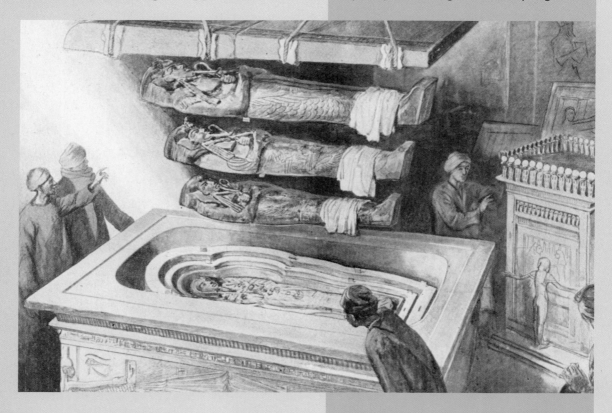

Egypt. Also attached to the front of the coffin are a crook (a stick used by shepherds) and a flail (a type of whip). The crook and flail were symbols of the pharaoh. This is King Tut!

Carter notices the coffin's size, and his heart races. It is huge—more than 7 feet (2 m) long. Why so big? There must be more coffins nested inside! Tomorrow the archaeologists will continue their work and find out.

COME BACK NEXT YEAR

As it turns out, Carter and his team do not find out what is in the coffin. Carter and Egyptian government officials have been arguing over the excavation site. Carter wants more control over the site. The officials want to decide who may or may not visit the tomb. The officials refuse to admit Carter's friends. At the same time, they allow crowds of important local people to visit the tomb. Carter claims these people are damaging the artifacts.

The last straw comes when Egyptian officials make new rules that take away more of Carter's authority. Carter quits work in the tomb. He goes home to England. His friends try to calm everyone down. They talk to Egyptian officials. Finally, late in 1924, the Egyptian government agrees to give Carter more control over the work.

In January 1925, Carter returns to Egypt. When he arrives at King Tut's tombs, he is very angry. People have been tramping in and out of the tomb. Objects have been moved and taken out of the tomb. One of King Tut's funeral cloths was even left outdoors. It is now ruined. Carter spends weeks cleaning up the tomb again. By then the weather is getting too hot to begin work. Carter and his team must wait until the fall.

BETTER AND BETTER

On October 13, Carter, Callender, and other archaeologists again gather around King Tut's coffin. They lift the lid. As Carter thought, the first coffin contains a second coffin. It is also built in the shape of a person and coated with gold foil. The figure on the second coffin also wears the pharaoh's headdress and carries a crook and flail. But this coffin is even more magnificent than the first. Red, blue, and turquoise glass and jewel-like stones decorate the surface.

Workers lift the lid of the second coffin. Excited gasps echo off the stone walls of the tomb. Carter's own heart almost stops beating. Inside is a third coffin, also shaped like a human body and dressed as a pharaoh.

"Absolutely incredible," Carter thought. This coffin is more than six feet long. It is not just coated in gold—it is made from solid gold. Its lid is decorated with jewels and carvings of Egyptian goddesses.

THE MUMMY'S GOLDEN MASK

Carter leans over and gets a grip on one side of the coffin's lid. Callender and two other archaeologists do the same. Between deep breaths, they tug on the lid. It is so heavy!

They expect something extraordinary. But no one is prepared for this sight. The mummy of King Tut lies inside. A fantastic solid gold mask gleams on the mummy's head. The mask shows King Tut's face. He is young and very handsome.

The strips of cloth, wrapped around King Tut so long ago, are gray and grimy. But sewn onto the mummy's wrappings are a pair of golden hands. They clasped remains of a crook and a flail. Below them is a big golden ba bird. It is the bird that carries King Tut's spirit back to the tomb.

Carter knows that a mummy's wrappings often contain jewels and other precious objects. The ancient Egyptians wrapped them into the mummy as charms to make sure the king lived on after death. Carter and the other archaeologists begin searching the wrappings for treasures. They find almost 150 jewels and other objects in the thirteen layers of the mummy's wrappings.

The archaeologists work with care. But they damage the mummy. For example, to remove bracelets from King Tut's wrists, the archaeologists cut off the mummy's hands.

More damage occurs as the workers try to remove the mummy from its coffin. King Tut's priests had poured a thick, sticky substance over the mummy once it was in the coffin. The substance hardened almost like tar. The mummy is stuck fast to the bottom of the coffin. Carter uses hot knives to melt the substance and dig out the mummy. But the knives destroy part of the mummy's back.

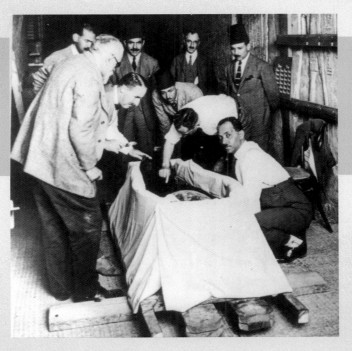

Howard Carter leans over King Tut's mummy with a magnifying glass as the first incision is made into the mummy's wrappings in early 1926.

UNDRESSING A MUMMY

The next step is to examine the naked mummy. Carter calls in physicians who do autopsies. An autopsy is an examination of a dead body to find out the cause of death. The doctors begin their work on November 11, 1925.

King Tut's autopsy also will give more information about exactly how the ancient Egyptians made a mummy. Carter finds telltale signs of King Tut's mummification. For instance, his fingers touch a cut in King Tut's stomach. The mummy makers used this cut to remove the pharaoh's stomach and intestines.

Examining the mummy gives the archaeologists other valuable information. Doctors can tell the age of a mummy from its teeth and bones. King Tut's teeth are in good condition. The doctors determine that King Tut died at about the age of eighteen. The doctors also learn that King Tut was short—about 5.5 feet (1.7 m) tall. And his head was bald. At eighteen King Tut would not naturally be bald. That is evidence that the Egyptians shaved their heads.

The autopsy cannot tell the archaeologists exactly how King Tut had died. Judging from his bones and teeth, he had been healthy. But what about those rumors from 3,000 years ago? Did Ay or someone else kill Tut? If King Tut had been poisoned or strangled, his bones would not show the evidence. So what had killed the young pharaoh? Carter knows it will take more time and research to answer that question.

THE TREASURY

After the mummy autopsy, Carter returns King Tut's remains to a wooden box in the tomb. But his work at the tomb is not over. He must remove more objects from the other chambers.

With the burial chamber cleared, Carter and his team can begin work on the treasury. On October 24, 1926, they walked past the fierce stare of the Anubis statue into the room. They can hardly take their eyes off the golden shrine.

The shrine stands about 6.5 feet (2 m) tall. Carter can now see that there are four statues of goddesses around the shrine—one on each side. The goddesses are Selket, Nephthys, Neith, and Isis. They are called tutelary goddesses. *Tutelary* means that they are guardians.

Inside the shrine, Carter and his team find a large square object covered in a dark cloth. They remove the cloth to find a chest made of a cream-colored stone called calcite. Carter knows that this is the canopic chest.

These modern-day images show the canopic shrine (*left*) guarded by the Egyptian goddess Selket. A close-up view of Selket (*above*) shows the detail in the statue of the goddess.

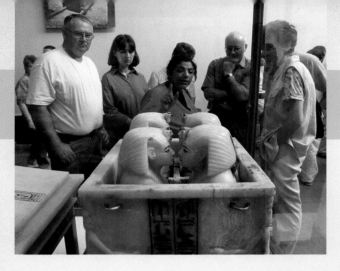

Visitors to the Egyptian Museum in Cairo can look at the canopic chest from King Tut's tomb and the four canopic jars inside.

When workers lift the chest's lid, they see four small heads carved from calcite. The heads are stoppers, or plugs, for four shafts hollowed out of the stone. Inside each hollow is a canopic jar—the jars used to keep King Tut's lungs, liver, stomach, and intestines. The four canopic jars are shaped like miniature versions of King Tut's coffins.

Carter looks through the other chests and small shrines that fill the treasury. He finds a small wooden chest that is not decorated. He opens it and finds two tiny coffins. The coffins contain the mummies of two infants. Carter realizes that King Tut and Queen Ankhesenamen had two daughters. One may have died while still in her mother's womb. The other may have died soon after birth.

HOMEWARD BOUND

Carter and the other archaeologists finish photographing and recording everything they find in the treasury and the annex. By November 1930, the last objects have been removed from the tomb. For several more months, Carter studies and conserves (repairs and protects) the objects. In March 1932, Carter finishes his work. The contents of King Tut's tomb are shipped to the Egyptian Museum in Cairo. Most are put on display for people to see.

Carter can hardly believe it. Almost ten years have passed since discovery of those sixteen steps that led to the most extraordinary Egyptian tomb ever found.

Carter says his good-byes to all the workers and friends who have helped him. With his notebooks, drawings, and photographs, he boards a ship bound for England. Already, he is thinking about writing books on his experiences in the Valley of the Kings.

Crowds gather outside the Field Museum in Chicago, Illinois, in 2006 for the opening of the exhibit "Tutankhamen and the Golden Age of the Pharaohs." Exhibits featuring artifacts from King Tut's tomb have traveled around the world.

EPILOGUE

King Tut, ancient Egypt, and mummies remained popular in books and movies long after Carter's discovery. Scientists also remain interested in King Tut. One unanswered question was how the young king had died. Some archaeologists thought that an enemy murdered King Tut by bashing him on the head. That idea began to spread in 1968, after scientists examined King Tut's mummy with X-rays. The X-ray pictures showed that a bone in part of King Tut's skull was crushed.

In 1976 King Tut moved from the laboratory to center stage. The Egyptian Organization of Antiquities worked with six U.S. museums to bring a traveling King Tut exhibit to the United States. The museums displayed King Tut's treasures and original photographs of Carter's excavation.

Eight million people came to see the traveling exhibit. It caused another bout of "Tutmania." People were amazed at the beautiful gold treasures and Egyptian artifacts. They wanted to learn more about the boy king. Many wanted to visit Egypt. A U.S. comedian, Steve Martin, even wrote a song about King Tut and performed it on the popular TV show *Saturday Night Live*. King Tut was a celebrity once again.

MORE ANSWERS

People seemed to enjoy the mystery that surrounded King Tut. In addition to believing that he was murdered, some people still believed in the curse of King Tut. They thought that Lord Carnarvon and others had died mysteriously soon after the excavations at King Tut's tomb.

In 2002 scientists decided to test the legend of King Tut's curse. They studied the lives of people involved in opening King Tut's tomb and removing its contents. The study was published in the *British Medical Journal*. It found that most of these people actually had long lives. Lady Evelyn Herbert, for example, lived until 1980—fifty-eight years after the discovery of King Tut's tomb.

In January 2005, scientists also took another look at the idea that King Tut was murdered. They studied King Tut's mummy with an advanced type of X-ray called a CT (computerized tomography) scan. Computerized tomography uses X-ray photos to create a three-dimensional image of a body. Scientists used the scanner to take 1,700 X-ray pictures of King Tut's mummy from head to toe.

The CT scans showed that King Tut's head probably was damaged after his death. They also showed that King Tut had a broken bone in his left leg. King Tut may have died from that broken leg. If the broken leg caused a serious infection, King Tut's doctors would have had no drugs that could treat it. He might have died from the infection.

The CT scans could not prove that King Tut was not murdered. For example, he might have been poisoned. Traces of poison would not show up on a CT scan of the mummy. But the scans did go a long way in proving that King Tut was not hit on the head. And they offer a good explanation of what might have happened.

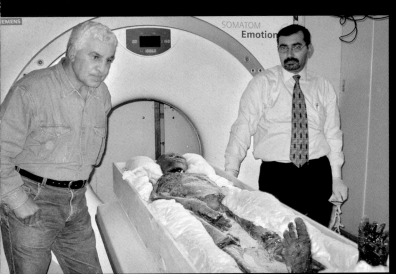

Zahi Hawass *(left)*, Egypt's leading archaeologist, and a researcher *(right)* stand with King Tut's mummy outside a CT scanner in 2005. The scanner took 1,700 images of the mummy for scientists to study.

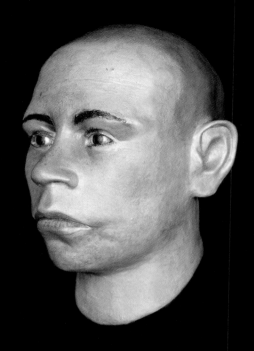

This facial reconstruction of King Tut's head was done in 2002 by a group of British experts. They reconstructed his features using X-rays of his skull.

THE PHARAOH'S FACE

Scientists also realized that the CT scans of the mummy's head could help re-create King Tut's facial features. Such a project would show the modern world what King Tut had really looked like. Three teams of scientists from Egypt, the United States, and France began working separately on the project. Scientists on all three teams were experts at reconstructing, or rebuilding, faces from skulls.

The French team was told that it was re-creating King Tut's face. To create the face, the team first used the CT scans to make a model of the skull. They took many detailed measurements of the skull model. The measurements helped the scientists know how to fit "skin" over the skull. In this case, they sculpted clay over the skull to create a lifelike face.

The U.S. team was given a copy of the model skull. But they were not told that the skull belonged to King Tut. They did not even know the sex, age, or race of their subject. By studying the skull, however, the scientists came up with some very important information. They knew that their subject was male and that he was in his late teens. They also decided that he was Caucasoid—a race common in North Africa, the Middle East, India, and Europe. The U.S. team then used more measurements from the skull to create a face, as the French team had.

The third team, Egyptian scientists, also knew they were re-creating King Tut's face. They created a model skull and covered it in clay to create the face.

The teams then compared their reconstructed faces. Even though they had worked separately, the results were very similar. And Egyptian experts agreed that the reconstructed face looked very much like portraits of King Tut made when he was a young teen.

KING TUT'S TRAVELS

King Tut's tomb has helped make people more aware of great civilizations of the past. King Tut's tomb contained about 3,500 objects. Millions of modern people have seen those objects in pictures and films. Some have seen King Tut's treasures in person at the Egyptian Museum in Cairo or at traveling exhibitions around the world.

King Tut's tomb has helped us understand more about the great civilization of ancient Egypt.

Visitors view and take photographs of King Tut's golden coffin, on display in 2005 at the Los Angeles County Museum of Art in California.

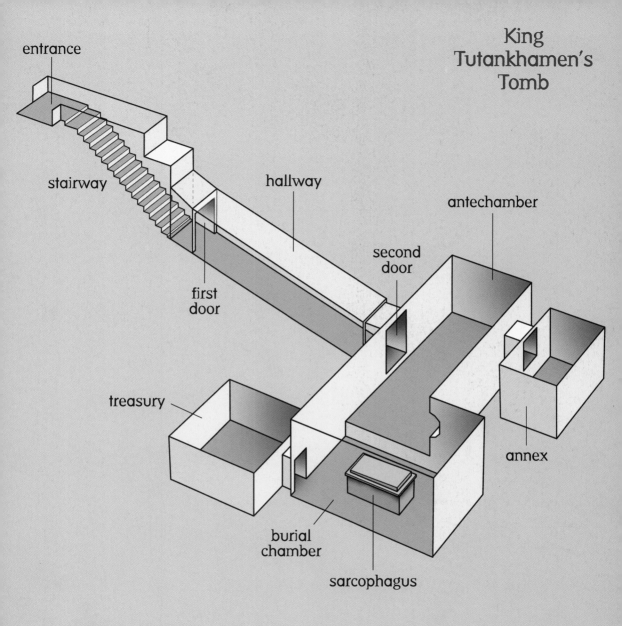

King Tutankhamen's Tomb

entrance

stairway

hallway

first door

second door

antechamber

treasury

annex

burial chamber

sarcophagus

King Tutankhamen's tomb was designed like most royal tombs of its day. A staircase and a long hallway led to rooms filled with treasures. Tutankhamen's mummy was found inside a sarcophagus located within gold shrines in the burial chamber.

TIMELINE

CA. 1334 B.C.
Tutankhamen becomes Egypt's pharaoh at the age of nine.

CA. 1325 B.C.
King Tut dies at the age of eighteen, after only nine years of being king.

1000 B.C.
Ramses VI's tomb is built. King Tut's tomb is buried beneath the building rubble.

A.D. 1891
Howard Carter begins work in the Valley of the Kings at the age of seventeen.

1900
The Egyptian government hires Carter as one of its chief archaeologists.

1907
Theodore Davis finds a piece of gold foil, which he thinks is from King Tut's tomb.

1914
Davis stops work in the Valley of the Kings.

1917
Carter and Lord Carnarvon start digging for King Tut's tomb in the Valley of the Kings.

1922
After years of finding nothing, Lord Carnarvon agrees to pay for one more year of excavations. Late in the year, Carter discovers King Tut's tomb. News of the discovery spreads around the world.

1923
Carter and his team of workers reveal the burial chamber and shrine to visitors. After the excavation season ends, Lord Carnarvon dies from a blood infection. Late in the year, Carter begins taking apart the burial shrine.

1924
Carter removes the lid to King Tut's sarcophagus. But further work on the tomb stops after Carter argues with the Egyptian government.

1925
Carter goes back to work in Egypt. He and his team remove the coffins from the sarcophagus and uncover King Tut's mummy. Doctors autopsy the mummy to try to learn the cause of death.

1926

Carter and his team enter the treasury. They discover King Tut's canopic jars inside a golden shrine.

1930

The last objects are removed from King Tut's tomb. Carter continues to study and conserve the objects.

1932

The last of King Tut's treasures are moved to the Egyptian Museum in Cairo.

1939

Carter dies in England at the age of sixty-four.

1968

Scientists X-ray King Tut's mummy. The X-rays show that the king might have been murdered by a blow to the head.

1976

The Egyptian Organization of Antiquities and U.S. museums arrange an exhibit of King Tut's treasures. The exhibit tours six U.S. cities. Eight million people come to see the exhibit.

2002

Scientists test the legend of King Tut's curse. They discover that most of the people involved in the tomb excavation lived average length or long lives.

2005

A CT scan reveals that the damage to King Tut's skull was probably caused after his death. Scientists use the skull and CT scans to create a 3-D image of what King Tut probably looked like.

"Tutankhamun and the Golden Age of the Pharaohs," an exhibit of treasures from King Tut's tomb and other eighteenth dynasty tombs, begins its U.S. tour.

2007

Zahi Hawass and a team of Egyptian archaeologists discover eight baskets of 3,000-year-old fruit in King Tut's tomb. For the first time, the face of King Tut's mummy is uncovered and displayed to the public in a climate-controlled glass box within his tomb.

PRONUNCIATION GUIDE

Ancient Egyptians spoke Egyptian. Egyptian belongs to the Afro-Asiatic family of languages. For many centuries, these languages have been spoken across northern Africa and southwest Asia. The Egyptian language died out in the 1600s. Most modern Egyptians speak another Afro-Asiatic language, Egyptian Arabic.

Below is a pronunciation key to the personal names and place-names used in the text:

Ankhesenamen	ahnk-ehs-ehn-AH-muhn
Anubis	uh-NOO-buhs
Ay	EYE
Hatshepsut	HAT-shep-soot
Horemheb	hawr-EM-hehb
Horus	HAWR-us
Isis	EYE-sis
Neith	NEETH
Nephthys	NEHF-thihs
Selket	SEHL-keht
Suppuluiumas	SUP-peh-loo-lee-mahs
Thebes	THEEBZ
Tutankhamen	too-tahng-KAH-muhn
Zannanza	za-NAHN-zah

GLOSSARY

afterlife: life after death. People who believe in an afterlife believe that some part of a person, such as their spirit, lives on after death.

akh: in ancient Egyptian religion, a person born again into the afterlife. If a dead person is properly mummified and laid to rest, the ka and ba reunite with the physical body to become the akh.

annex: a storage room next to the antechamber in King Tut's tomb

antechamber: the first room discovered in King Tut's tomb

archaeologist: a scientist who studies buildings, tools, pottery, and other objects used by humans in the past

artifact: objects or the remains of objects made by people who lived in the past

ba: in ancient Egyptian religion, the spirit that returns to a person's body after death

burial chamber: the room in King Tut's tomb that contained his mummy

canopic jar: a special container used to preserve the internal organs after they are removed from the body during mummification

cobra: a poisonous snake found in Africa and Asia. In ancient Egypt, the cobra was a symbol of the pharaoh's rule over Lower Egypt (the northern part of the kingdom).

crook: a stick with a curved handle used by shepherds to guide their flocks. In ancient Egypt, the crook was a symbol of the pharaoh's royalty.

CT (computerized tomography) scan: a special X-ray exam of the body that can show certain injuries and diseases

dig: the word archaeologists use for a search for buried artifacts

dynasty: a family of rulers

Egyptology: the study of ancient Egypt

excavation: the process of exposing something by digging it up

falcon: a large bird related to the hawk and the eagle. To the ancient Egyptians, the falcon was a symbol of the god Horus.

flail: a whip. Ancient Egyptian flails were rods with three strands of beads attached to the end. They were symbols of the pharaoh's royalty.

hieroglyphics (hy-ruh-GLIH-fiks): a system of writing that uses pictures (hieroglyphs) instead of letters

ka: in ancient Egyptian religion, a person's life force

mummy: the body of a person or animal preserved in a certain way

natron: a salt used during mummification to preserve a dead body

pharaoh (FAIR-oh): a king or ruler in ancient Egypt

sarcophagus (sahr-KAH-fuh-guhs): a stone coffin that often holds another smaller coffin

shrine: a holy object or place

tomb: a burial place

treasury: a storage room next to the burial chamber in King Tut's tomb

tutelary: acting as a guardian

Valley of the Kings: a desert area west of the Nile River where ancient Egyptians buried their pharaohs

vizier: an adviser to the pharaoh

vulture: a large bird. In ancient Egypt, the vulture was a symbol of the pharaoh's rule over Upper Egypt (the southern part of the kingdom).

WHO'S WHO?

Lord Carnarvon (1866–1923) was born George Edward Stanhope Molyneux Herbert. He grew up on his family's estate, Highclere, in southern England. As an older man, Carnarvon's health was not good. He began spending winters in Egypt to escape the cold, damp English weather. He became interested in archaeology and met Howard Carter. He provided the money for Carter's search for and excavation of King Tut's tomb. Without Carnarvon's support, Carter probably would not have discovered King Tut's tomb. Carnarvon died on April 5, 1923, of an infected mosquito bite. His unexpected death helped spread the idea of King Tut's curse.

Howard Carter (1874–1939) was born in London, England. As a young child, Howard became interested in art. His father, Samuel John Carter, was a well-known artist who painted pictures of animals. Howard also liked to read about ancient Egypt.

Those interests led Howard to Egypt when he was only seventeen years old. Howard was hired by archaeologists to make drawings of tombs, temples, and objects. While working, Howard learned Egyptian Arabic, the language most widely spoken in Egypt. He also learned a great deal about archaeology.

In 1900 the Egyptian government hired Carter as one of its chief archaeologists. Carter worked on some of the first excavations in the Valley of the Kings. Carter later met Lord Carnarvon, a wealthy Englishman who often visited Egypt and was interested in archaeology. The two agreed to work together. In 1917 they started digging in the Valley of the Kings for the tomb of King Tut.

On November 4, 1922, Carter discovered the tomb. Carter spent the next ten years discovering, preserving, and studying objects from King Tut's tomb. After finishing that work in 1932, Carter wrote books on King Tut and gave speeches about his great discoveries.

Theodore M. Davis (1837–1915) was a wealthy American lawyer who took up Egyptology as a hobby. In the early 1900s, Davis began excavations in Egypt's Valley of the Kings. In 1907 Davis and his team uncovered an underground chamber in the valley. The chamber contained artifacts that belonged to King Tut, but the team could not find King Tut's tomb. In fact, they were only about 3 feet (1 m) away from the tomb. Davis later stopped excavating in the valley, declaring that all the great ancient Egyptian tombs had been discovered. Several years later, Carter began excavating in the same area and discovered King Tut's real tomb.

SOURCE NOTES

9 Howard Carter, quoted in Erik Hornung, *The Valley of the Kings: Horizon of Eternity*, trans. David Warburton (New York: Timken Publishers, 1990), 17.

11 Hornung, *The Valley of the Kings: Horizon of Eternity*, 40.

17 Zahi Hawass, *Tutankhamen: The Mystery of the Boy King* (Washington, DC: National Geographic, 2005), 59.

21 Thomas Hoving, *Tutankhamen: The Untold Story* (New York: Simon and Schuster, 1978), 50.

21 Ibid.

21 Ibid.

23 Larry Orcutt, *Catchpenny Mysteries* (n.d.), http://www.catchpenny.org/curses.html (April 30, 2006).

24 Howard Carter and A.C. Mace, *The Discovery of the Tomb of Tutankhamen* (1923; repr., New York: Dover Publications, 1977), 86.

25 T. G. H. James, *Howard Carter: The Path to Tutankhamen* (London: Tauris Parke Paperbacks, 1992), 252.

26 Carter and Mace, *The Discovery of the Tomb of Tutankhamen*, 87.

27 Ibid., 90.

29 Ibid., 94.

29 James, *Howard Carter*, 252.

32 Carter and Mace, *The Discovery of the Tomb of Tutankhamen*, 95.

32 Ibid., 99.

38 Howard Carter and A. C. Mace, *The Tomb of Tut Ankh Amen*, vol. 1, *Search, Discovery, and Clearance of the Antechamber* (1923; repr., London: Gerald Duckworth, 2003), 76.

38 Hoving, *Tutankhamen*, 122.

40 Carter and Mace, *The Discovery of the Tomb of Tutankhamen*, 105.

41 James, *Howard Carter*, 275.

43 Nicholas Reeves, *The Complete Tutankhamen* (New York: Thames and Hudson, 1990), 82.

44 Carter and Mace, *The Tomb of Tut Ankh Amen*, vol. 1, 196.

46 Hoving, *Tutankhamen*, 197.

48 Carter and Mace, *The Tomb of Tut Ankh Amen*, vol. 1, 204.

52 Reeves, *The Complete Tutankhamen*, 100.

52 Ibid., 105.

54 Ibid., 106.

56 Hoving, *Tutankhamen*, 360.

SELECTED BIBLIOGRAPHY

Carter, Howard, and A.C. Mace. *The Discovery of the Tomb of Tutankhamen*. 1923. Reprint, New York: Dover Publications, 1977.

Doherty, Paul. *The Mysterious Death of Tutankhamen*. New York: Carroll & Graf, 2002.

El Mahdy, Christine. *Tutankhamen: The Life and Death of the Boy-King*. New York: St. Martin's Press, 1999.

Hawass, Zahi. *The Golden Age of Tutankhamen*. Cairo: American University of Cairo Press, 2004.

Hornung, Erik. *The Valley of the Kings: Horizon of Eternity*. Translated by David Warburton. New York: Timken Publishers, 1990.

Hoving, Thomas. *Tutankhamen: The Untold Story*. New York: Simon and Schuster, 1978.

James, T. G. H. *Howard Carter: The Path to Tutankhamen*. London: Tauris Parke Paperbacks, 1992.

O'Brien, Alexandra A. "Death in Ancient Egypt." *Oriental Institute Research Archives*. 1999. http://www-oi.uchicago.edu/OI/DEPT/RA/ABZU/DEATH.HTML (November 9, 2007).

Reeves, Nicholas, and Richard H. Wilkinson. *The Complete Valley of the Kings: Tombs and Treasures of Egypt's Greatest Pharaohs*. London: Thames and Hudson, 1996.

Roehrig, Catharine H. *Explorers and Artists in the Valley of the Kings*. Cairo: American University in Cairo Press, 2002.

Schulz, Regine, and Matthias Seidel, eds. *Egypt: The World of the Pharaohs*. Koln, DEU: Konemann, 1998.

Silverman, David P., ed. *Ancient Egypt*. New York: Oxford University Press, 1997.

Vandenberg, Philipp. *The Golden Pharaoh*. New York: Macmillan, 1980.

FURTHER READING AND WEBSITES

BOOKS

Caselli, Giovanni. *In Search of Tutankhamen: The Discovery of a King's Tomb*. New York: Peter Bedrick Books, 2001.

Day, Nancy. *Your Travel Guide to Ancient Egypt*. Minneapolis: Twenty-First Century Books, 2001.

Hawass, Zahi. *Tutankhamen: The Mystery of the Boy King*. Washington, DC: National Geographic Children's Books, 2005.

McCall, Henrietta. *Gods and Goddesses in the Daily Life of Ancient Egyptians*. New York: Peter Bedrick Books, 2002.

Steedman, Scott. *History News: The Egyptian News*. Milwaukee: Gareth Stevens, 2000.

Wilcox, Charlotte. *Mummies, Bones, & Body Parts*. Minneapolis: Carolrhoda Books, 2000.

———. *Mummies & Their Mysteries*. Minneapolis: Carolrhoda Books, 1993.

WEBSITES

Ancient Egypt

http://www.ancientegypt.co.uk/menu.html

This website, created by the British Museum, explains life in ancient Egypt—from the geography of the Nile basin to what people did for a living.

Ancient Egypt Timeline

http://www.bbc.co.uk/history/ancient/egyptians/timeline.shtml

This website lists important dates in ancient Egyptian history from 3100 B.C. to A.D. 395. Part of the British Broadcasting Corporation's ancient history site, it also provides links to more information on King Tut and the treasures found in his tomb.

At the Tomb of Tutankhamen

http://www.nationalgeographic.com/egypt/

Read an online version of the original February 1923 *National Geographic* article detailing the opening of King Tut's tomb.

Dig

http://www.digonsite.com/drdig/egypt/index.html

Dig, an online archaeology magazine for students, features an archaeology quiz, glossary, factoids, and links to archaeology websites. Its Ask Dr. Dig column answers many questions about ancient Egypt and King Tut.

The Plateau

http://www.guardians.net/hawass/

Egyptian archaeologist Zahi Hawass is the secretary general of the Supreme Council of Antiquities in Egypt. His English-language website features news about ongoing work in the Valley of the Kings, information about CT scans of mummies, and articles about Egyptian history. The many photographs of mummies and of archaeologists in action may intrigue younger readers.

The Theban Mapping Project

http://www.thebanmappingproject.com/

The Theban Mapping Project shows readers all the Valley of the Kings tombs in relation to one another. Interactive map features lead into the tombs, complete with three-dimensional models and short movies.

Unravelling the Mysteries of King Tutankhamen

http://magma.nationalgeographic.com/ngm/tut/mysteries/index.html

The *National Geographic* magazine's online archive includes this June 2005 issue on King Tut. The article features an interactive expedition into the tomb and a link to the 2005 facial reconstruction project.

INDEX

ABOUT THE AUTHORS

Michael Woods is a science and medical journalist in Washington, D.C. He has won many national writing awards. Mary B. Woods is a school librarian. Their past books include the eight-volume Ancient Technology series and the fifteen-part Disasters Up Close series. The Woodses have four children. When not writing, reading, or enjoying their grandchildren, they travel to gather material for future books.

PHOTO ACKNOWLEDGMENTS

The images in this book are used with permission of: © SuperStock, Inc./SuperStock, p. 4; The Art Archive/Luxor Museum, Egypt/Dagli Orti, p. 5; © age fotostock/SuperStock, p. 6; © Laura Westlund/Independent Picture Service, pp. 7, 65; © General Photographic Agency/Hulton Archive/Getty Images, p. 9; © Kurt Scholz/SuperStock, p. 10; © Peter Willi/SuperStock, p. 12; The Art Archive/Egyptian Museum Cairo/Dagli Orti, pp. 13, 33, 44; © Darren Erickson/Independent Picture Service, p. 14; © Bridgeman Art Library, London/SuperStock, p. 16; © Roger Viollet/Getty Images, p. 18; © Hulton Archive/Getty Images, pp. 20, 27, 40 (bottom right), 53; © Giraudon/Art Resource, NY, p. 21; Library of Congress, pp. 22 (LC-USZ62-134403), 30–31 (LC-USZ62-134415), 57 (LC-USZ62-60946); © English Heritage/HIP/The Image Works, p. 24; © Lord Carnarvon/Mansell/Time Life Pictures/Getty Images, p. 25; © Stapleton Collection/CORBIS, p. 28; The Art Archive/Pharaonic Village Cairo/Dagli Orti, pp. 34, 47 (left); © Ralph Notaro/Getty Images, pp. 36, 52; AP Photo, p. 39; © Mary Evans Picture Library, pp. 40 (top), 54; © Francois Guenet/Art Resource, NY, pp. 40 (bottom left), 47 (right), 48; © Gustavo Caballero/Getty Images, p. 41; The Illustrated London News, p. 42; © Scala/Art Resource, NY, p. 45; © Roger Wood/CORBIS, pp. 46, 58 (right); © Ethan Miller/Getty Images, p. 50; © akg-images, p. 51; © Silvio Fiore/SuperStock, p. 58 (left); © Sandro Vannini/CORBIS, p. 59; AP Photo/M. Spencer Green, p. 60; AP Photo/Saedi Press, p. 62; © Guy Levy/epa/CORBIS, p. 63; AP Photo/Ric Francis, p. 64.

Cover: © Rosemary Calvert/Photographer's Choice/Getty Images.